Merry Christmas

The Night Before Christmas *Adapted by Keith Dixon*	3
The Robin and the Snowman *Written by Keith Dixon*	11
Minstrel Mouse and the Jingle Bells *Written by Michael Dunn*	20
When Santa got Stuck up the Chimney *Written by Karen Fox*	31

A fully illustrated CYP book

The Night Before Christmas *Adapted by Keith Dixon*

'Twas the night before Christmas, when all through the house
Not a creature was stirring, not even a mouse;
The stockings were hung by the chimney with care,
In hopes that St Nicholas soon would be there.

The children were nestled all snug in their beds,
While visions of sugar-plums danced in their heads;
And mamma in her 'kerchief, and I in my cap,
Had just settled down for a long winter's nap.

When out on the lawn there arose such a clatter,
I sprang from the bed to see what was the matter.
Away to the window I flew like a flash,
Tore open the shutters and threw up the sash.

The moon on the breast of the new-fallen snow,
Gave the lustre of mid-day to objects below;
When, what to my wandering eyes should appear,
But a miniature sleigh, and eight tiny reindeer.

4

With a little old driver, so lively and quick,
I knew in a moment it must be St. Nick.
More rapid than eagles his coursers they came,
And he whistled, and shouted, and called them by name;

"Now, Dasher! Now, Dancer! Now, Prancer and Vixen!
On, Comet! On, Cupid! On, Donder and Blitzen!
To the top of the porch! To the top of the wall!
Now dash away! Dash away! Dash away! All!"

As dry leaves before the wild hurricane fly,
When they meet with an obstacle, mount to the sky,
So up to the house-top the coursers they flew,
With the sleigh full of toys, and St Nicholas too.

And then in a twinkling I heard on the roof,
The prancing and pawing of each little hoof.
As I drew in my hand and was turning around,
Down the chimney St Nicholas came with a bound.

He was dressed all in fur, from his head to his foot,
And his clothes were all tarnished with ashes and soot;
A bundle of toys he had flung on his back,
And he looked like a peddler just opening his pack.

His eyes - how they twinkled! His dimples how merry!
His cheeks were like roses, his nose like a cherry!
His droll little mouth was drawn up in a bow,
And the beard on his chin was as white as the snow.

He was chubby and plump, a right jolly old elf,
And I laughed when I saw him, in spite of myself;
A wink of his eye, and a twist of his head,
Soon gave me to know I had nothing to dread.

He spoke not a word, but went straight to his work,
And filled all the stockings; then turned with a jerk,
And laying his finger aside of his nose,
And giving a nod, up the chimney he rose.

He sprang to his sleigh, to his team gave a whistle,
And away they all flew like the down of a thistle.
But I heard him exclaim, ere he drove out of sight,
"Happy Christmas to all, and to all a good-night!"

10

The Robin and the Snowman *Written by Keith Dixon*

It was two days before Christmas and Chloe and Hayley were excited. They had just decorated the Christmas tree with lights, tinsel and sparkling decorations. Sat on top of the tree was their special Christmas fairy.

Suddenly their dog, Casey, ran into the room and straight into the tree, sending it crashing to the floor. Mum appeared and began to pick it up, but the girls saw the fairy lying on the floor, broken into lots of tiny pieces.

"I'm very sorry girls, but it is too badly broken to be repaired," said Mum. The girls were very upset.

"It's been snowing," said Mum. "Why don't you go and build a snowman in the garden? That would be fun!"

Watching from outside the window was Ronald, a little robin redbreast. He loved the girls, as they always made sure he had plenty of food to eat.

"I've got to do something to make the girls happy again for Christmas," he chirped.

The girls spent the whole day building a big snowman, using a carrot for his nose and black pebbles from the flowerbeds for his eyes and mouth. They put an old hat on the top of his head and tied a scarf around his neck. Then, when they had finished, the girls went inside as it was time for their tea.

When the girls had gone, Ronald the robin flew down and landed on the snowman's shoulder. The snowman opened his eyes, looked at Ronald and said, "You look sad for such a beautiful little bird."

"I am sad for my friends, the girls who made you," said Ronald. "Their Christmas fairy decoration is broken and they are very upset. It is Christmas and they should be happy. I want to do something to help, but I can't think of anything!"

"I've got an idea," said the snowman.

He bent down, scooped up some snow and put it under his hat. Ronald watched as the snowman closed his eyes and concentrated. Suddenly there was a flash of bright light. When it had faded the snowman opened his eyes.

"What do you think of this?" asked the snowman as he took off his hat. "It's for the top of the girls' tree and it won't melt in the house because of special snowman magic!"

On his head sat the biggest, whitest and most sparkly snowflake that Ronald had ever seen. He was very happy.

Ronald flew to the dustbin and pulled out a plastic bag that was sticking out the top. He pecked the letters C and H into the front of the bag, carefully put the snowflake into it, and left it on the doorstep of the house for their mum to find.

The next morning it was Christmas Eve. Mum opened the door to bring in the milk and found the bag. When Mum saw the letters that Ronald had pecked into the bag she knew it was for the girls. She gave them the bag and they pulled out the giant snowflake.

"Wow!" they cried.

The beautiful snowflake was soon sitting on the top of the tree ready for Christmas Day, and it looked beautiful.

In the garden, Ronald watched the girls through the window from his nest. He was a very happy little robin. He smiled at his new friend the snowman and they wished each other, "Merry Christmas!"

Minstrel Mouse and the Jingle Bells

Written by Michael Dunn

Minstrel Mouse was very excited. It was the day before Christmas and he had spent many hours decorating his room at The Old Music Hall. The glittering Christmas tree, although small, looked very pretty. Minstrel had been wearing his Christmas hat all day.

Just as Minstrel settled down in his rocking chair for a well-deserved thimble of tea, the telephone rang. It made him jump and he nearly toppled off his rocking chair.

"Who can that be?" he wondered as he picked up the receiver. "Hello…?" said Minstrel.

"Ahh, Minstrel!" replied a great booming voice, "you're there, good lad. It's Santa Claus. How are you my little friend?"

"I'm fine thank you, Santa," replied Minstrel.

"Now, can you help me?" asked Santa. "The elves have spent all day wrapping presents and loading the sleigh. I've been organising everything. The reindeer are dressed up and ready to go... but we have a problem."

"Oh, oh dear!" said Minstrel.

"Yes, oh dear indeed. In fact, oh HO!" laughed Santa.

"Whatever is the matter?" asked Minstrel.

"Well, I was doing the routine check before take off. Presents... check, reindeer... check, but when I tested the jingle bells, there weren't any!" said Santa.

"Weren't any what?" asked Minstrel.

"Any jingles, Minstrel."

"Oh!" said Minstrel. "Oh dear."

"Oh HO!" replied Santa.

"Now, I know you're the most musical mouse in the world, and I thought, if anyone has any jingles, Minstrel has. So I telephoned straight away," explained Santa. "Well, Minstrel, have you got any?"

"Ummm, now let me think," said Minstrel. "I've got some twangs, and I've got lots of rings and dings, but jingles… umm, I'll have to have a look."

"Right, come along then Minstrel, please look straight away," said Santa. "If I don't get these jingles soon, I'm going to be late delivering the toys to all the girls and boys."

"Okay, Santa, I'll call you back," replied Minstrel. "Speak to you later."

Minstrel put the phone down. "Now, let me think," he mused.

Minstrel did his best thinking when he was rocking back and forth in his rocking chair. He had a special hat too – his Thinking Cap. He went to his hat cupboard, found his Thinking Cap, and put it on.

"Ahh yes, I remember!" exclaimed Minstrel. He leaped off his rocking chair and went to his Magical Musical Cupboard. It was so big that Minstrel could creep inside and wander around. On the shelves there were lots of boxes with labels on - whistles, rings, trings, jangles – but no jingles.

Then, as he was wandering along one of the shelves, he tripped

"Agh!" he cried, as he fell over and bumped his nose.

"What was that?" There on the shelf was a jingle, only one, but it was a clue. Minstrel looked up. High on the top shelf he could see an old box. Written on the outside was 'Jingles – Special Christmas Jingles.'

"Ahh ha!" said Minstrel triumphantly.

Minstrel scurried up to the very top shelf of the cupboard and opened the box. Inside there were lots of Christmas jingles. It was just what Santa Claus needed. Minstrel Mouse climbed back down and telephoned Santa Claus straight away.

"Minstrel, that's marvellous!" said Santa excitedly. "I'll collect the jingles from you and then deliver all the presents."

Minstrel Mouse waited happily for Santa Claus to arrive. He had to listen very carefully because Santa's sleigh didn't have any jingles. Santa soon arrived.

"There you are Santa, a big box of jingles!" said Minstrel, holding out the box.

"Thank you, Minstrel, that's wonderful," said Santa. "I'll sprinkle them over the bells and we shall be off." Santa sprinkled busily. "There we are! I tell you what, Minstrel, why don't you come with us?"

"That would be wonderful!" exclaimed Minstrel as a big smile spread across his face. "I'll be in the sleigh with Santa, delivering all the gifts to the girls and boys. That's the best Christmas present I could ever have. Oh HO!"

"Oh yes," said Santa, "Oh HO!"

30

When Santa got Stuck up the Chimney

Written by Karen Fox

It was Christmas Eve. Throughout the night, Santa Claus, Rudolph and the other reindeer worked to deliver presents to all the good little boys and girls across the land.

"Through wind, snow, cold and rain, Christmas has arrived again!" yelled Santa with joy as he soared through the night sky on his sleigh.

Rudolph the reindeer's big red nose shone brightly in the moonlight. It lit up the sky like a flare, and guided the sleigh on its long journey across the snow and ice.

Mince pies were eaten, brandy sipped and carrots munched all the way from China to England. As the long night drew to a close, the sleigh landed on the roof of the final house on Santa's round. Tiptoeing over to the chimney top, Santa peered down it.

"Hmm," he whispered to Rudolph. "Very narrow it appears, this chimney flue, but no matter at all, it will have to do," and with a hop and a jump, Santa threw himself head first into the chimney. He shuffled down the chimneystack, pushing his sack in front of him until it hit the fireplace below with a soft thud.

"Now, if I just wriggle and jiggle a little bit more," he thought, "I can follow my sack right down to the floor," but however much he wriggled and jiggled, Santa just couldn't move. His arms and legs waved but his belly wouldn't budge an inch. Santa was stuck up the chimney!

Suddenly he heard the joyful sound of children's laughter coming from the fireside below. Then a boy's face appeared, wide-eyed and open-mouthed, staring up the chimney at Santa Claus.

"Santa's got stuck up the chimney!" said the boy to his brother and sisters, who were sitting by the Christmas tree waiting to see what had happened.

A few moments passed, during which there was hushed whispers and giggling. Santa grew worried that the children might think they were dreaming. Then they would return to bed, leaving him stuck up the chimney all night! So he began to shout,

"You girls and boys won't get any toys if you don't pull me out!"

There was silence, and Santa Claus wondered if they had gone back to bed after all. Feeling rather sorry for himself he shook the soot out of his beard and sniffled,

"My beard is black, there's soot on my sack, my nose is tickly too!"

Then he let out the biggest batch of sneezes anyone had ever heard.

"Aichoo, aichoo, aichoo!"

Luckily, the enormous sneezes dislodged Santa's belly and he fell with a clatter onto the fireplace. Then he rolled like a big red ball, out of the fireplace and onto the carpet. He stood up and dusted the soot from his red suit. He was about to pick up his sack when he noticed four small children gazing up at him in disbelief. Then one of the girls began to cry.

"Santa, we were going to pull you out," she moaned, "and now we won't get any toys!"

Realising that what their sister said was true, the other children also looked very sad.

Santa knelt down and bundled them all up in his arms.

"Well now," he said, "good boys and girls you have been all these years, so here are your presents and no need for tears."

Santa placed a gift under the tree for each girl and boy, and waved them all off to bed. He made his way cheerfully out of the house and back up to the roof, where Rudolph and the other reindeer were waiting with the sleigh. Santa used the front door this time, however… better safe than sorry after all!